Chimeras

poems by

Clare Welsh

Finishing Line Press
Georgetown, Kentucky

Chimeras

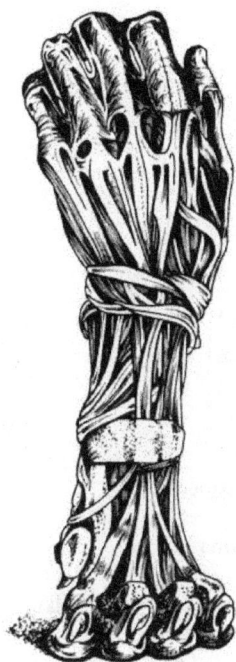

ACKNOWLEDGMENTS

A fluffy hug to the following publications, in which these poems, or versions
of them, first appeared:

The Susquehanna Review: "Parlor Nostalgia"
Pretty Owl Poetry: "Koi in a Shopping Mall Pond" and "Almost Exorcism"
The Axe Factory: "After the Apocalypse"
Viator: a longer version of "Be Prophecy", called "Opals"

All illustrations by the poet, Clare Welsh © 2015

Editor: Christen Kincaid

Cover Art: Clare Welsh

Author Photo: Shelby Ursu

Cover Design: Elizabeth Maines

Printed in the USA on acid-free paper.
Order online: www.finishinglinepress.com
          also available on amazon.com

Author inquiries and mail orders:
Finishing Line Press
P. O. Box 1626
Georgetown, Kentucky 40324
U. S. A.

Table of Contents

For anyone who woke up poorly put together

I

Beginnings
Ars Poetica

They bristle, bubble,
splinter, smell

of semen, petals,
mushrooms.

They're never
what you want

Now, This Way,
Here, not the babies

you asked for, these
chimeras. Tune them

taut, they are hot
strings humming

new songs, first songs,
the very first song

in the world was so
ugly the animals

buried their heads
in shit for a year

and your songs
are so, so much

uglier than that.
Love them. Love

you. Love you
loving your ugly songs

until this alchemy turns
all your shit to gold.

They Carried Horses

in the way horses
could not carry them:

In stories, songs, stamped in books
on The Iron Age, or else

in fluff-drunk speeches
about the day Dan

MacCába was flung in piles
of shit, how even the fleas

on the dog wouldn't
smooch his sticky beard,

and everyone had different
ways of telling how that

white mare shrugged his ass
from her ballet arch.

They carried horses across
Atlantic fevers, stuffed them

into cold Pittsburgh
apartments the way

other people stuffed secrets
behind lattice-lace curtains,

in silver-spoon rooms
of pregnant daughters.

They tried acting more Catholic
so they could produce more names

for the guilt that is
the churn of leaving

a hard life that is known for
a hard life that is not known,

they carried whole lives,
plopped them on bar stools

while they wrote cursive letters
to their past still steaming, red

as a tor island
that won't stop being

born, they drew a secret map
to future children showing

the way back, exact
patches of soil, peat

where we might place our ears,
hear the heft of hoof beats.

Aubade

When paintings receive
praise, I can't admit
art school was
an expensive excuse
to keep busy. I say some
shrugging half-truth:
Do anything for long enough
and you'll get good. Like the easy

Goodbye, all it takes
is practice. 7 AM ruffles
frayed prayer flags.
The dean at Tulane said
Tibetan Wind Horses
symbolize sprinting souls,
they will carry
my love for miles
so long as I drape rooms
in color. Outside,

hooves clop and echo:
mules tug brimming
carriages, mules because,
unlike horses, mules are
infertile. Docile. Willing
to trot the same six blocks
under the same cold whip
for years. 8 AM wafts

coffee, river water, oranges.
Every smell urges
be here. The man who left
his passport open
on my floor calls
from Colorado, I can't
put down my pen
long enough to answer. 9 AM,

and the morning
is long, but not as long
as what will come
after the morning.
In art school, teachers drew
circles in chalk, told me
time is distance. This life
consists of intersecting circles:
Mules rounding corners.
Horses rounding
bigger corners. People rounding
the Earth's diameter, embracing
or not embracing as they pass.
10 AM nudges early

drinkers to canal-side bars.
I think of joining them,
of keeping busy.
Sublimation is the process
by which we replace
old circles for new
circles. I broke

a circle once, everyone
saw. Friends still
talk about it, even the man
who left his passport
said, "I've heard
of you, naughty circle
breaker." It's embarrassing,
the way I jab elbows
into fat speech bubbles,
deflate expectations.
11 AM tugs me

inside. I'm looking
at paintings, telling myself
half-truths and laughing.
I couldn't laugh if it
were all true,
Dear God I promise
I'll never speak
whole truths Amen. 12 PM

shakes windows, chimes
a circle closing. The coda begs
repeat. Return
to prayer, to song,
to swelling, stretching
rituals of forgetting.

Parlor Nostalgia

The pictures here
cut deep.
      Indenting trails,
      the tattooing

needle plunges
like a hummingbird
      sipping in reverse
      so nectar surges

in—even
if these lines fade
      with sun, bloat
      with the salt

of living, wear them
like stories under skin,
      above rippling
      muscle. The past

is just another close
and colorful wound,
      a jeweled bird,
      a frayed banner,

a rose-haloed compass
with a magic arrow
      pointing the way
      back.

Be Prophecy

When strangers say, "you are
too much to trust,"
what they mean is

your eyes shine like teeth

so don't blink. Be
a staring prophecy.
Surpass that old
Delphian Oracle
who saw opals only
in the gaze of gyrating
women. Find the opals
buried under concrete,
the opals clutched
in the roots of palm trees
like candles jabbed between water
washed graves. Friend, these

instructions are as much for me
as they are for you. Ancient
minerals shoulder our highways.
Driving down the I-10 with hands
out the window, we paw at light
pollution, the city like Constantine's
opal crown. So what if
he was another
asshole in a fancy hat
trying to take our money?
We no longer get our news
from the Internet, we no longer
know which Emperors to hate.

The suburbs are fossils, their ribs
grid the wetlands. We step
from the car, place palms
to soil. Sinking in ferns
and petrified wood, we dig
through the smell of wet fur,
extract cataracts, milk
stones, find in each
other oracles.

Koi in a Shopping Mall Pond

Shaded under plastic trees, children
toss coins, zinc wafers fish gulp
then spit out,
as if to say
> *more worms, please*
>
> > *more earth*
> >
> > > *and slowness*

Chant for the Parasympathetic Nervous System

Come Kava, come Chamomile, come Passion
Flower crushed, rolled, inhaled with equal parts
Cannabis, exhaled with the city that chokes.
Come a good cough to know you're alive.
30 minutes of cardio, hot yoga, sweat
to flush the fear of what the body does
without permission. Come the humming
voice of an Internet Psychic: "What you need
is a place to unwind." Come the Great
Outdoors. *Come, come, I want you*
to come, says the salt-of-the-earth
lover in bed, come the fight
or flight stroked on each velvet ear,
the pulse slowed, the control
to stop controlling.

II.

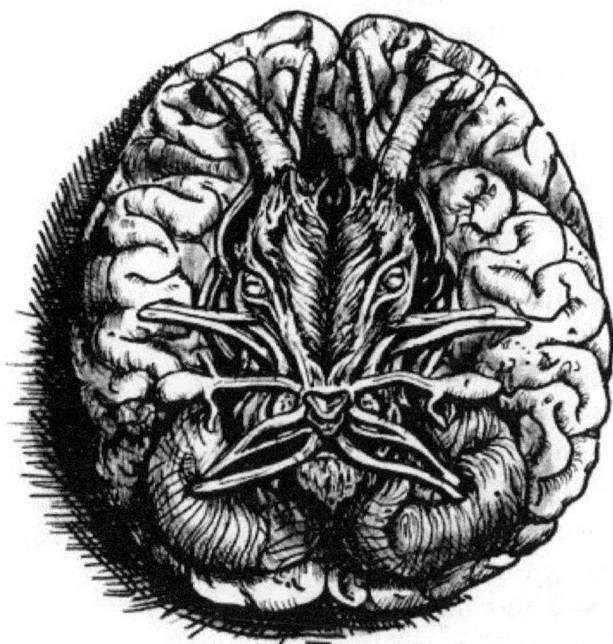

Roadside Attraction

The summer I ran
from all my problems, really
ran to black metal
crinkled by tangled headphones
as if another
Hail Satan could, by some law
of opposites make
me a better person—that
summer, mist thickened
around orange streetlights. I only
ran at night, only
to music that made me run
faster. Steam rose, hot
off the asphalt of country
roads. I passed the wet rot
of a dead stag, his white eyes
crusted with blood. Some
scavenger had sawed antler
crown from velvet skull.
I fantasized of ripping
open what was left,
of smearing my breasts and throat
with guts and flies. That
and sex. Sex inside of a dead deer
would, I thought, distract
me from bankruptcy, aging
parents, fluorescent
screens. While running I often
searched for distractions
to convince me I wasn't

running: a louder
sound than my breathing, the smear
of the Milky Way,
another scared animal.

The Swan

When it died, people from all over came to collect feathers, take pictures, or gape, phones in hand. One woman peered for ten minutes into the eye, a red disk the size of a tire. Before park rangers erected a fence around the body, children climbed the neck, grabbed fists of down. Pine trees were stapled with flyers urging people to take precautions against Avian Flu. No one noticed the smell—or the sound, a swarming of flies growing louder around the water. Plugging the entire lake, the body was bloated with tumors. A particularly bulbous cluster grew on the flesh between the skull and beak. A blogger for the local paper thought this made the face look reptilian, like a dragon. He took a selfie next to the partially exposed bone. Later, he deleted it: The light just wasn't right in the shadow of the carcass.

Almost Exorcism

A strange lump is found
on the ribs of a dog

1.

Children place their palms
on the dog, hands hovering
over the lump as if it is
a holy relic. They wonder
what the lump looks like
from the inside. Maybe

it is a second heart.
When one heart fails,
The other will push

air from wet
gooseflesh nose,
a howl from a husk,
maybe

when the dog cries
it is because he is
twice as hurt.

2.

One child
swears the lump
is a magic candy

stone that can make him

live forever.

He imagines cutting
the dog open
and living inside

a warm skin.

3.

The priest
sees children holding
down a dog, one child
holding a knife,
the priest breaks
them apart, says

the lump
is a sleuth of cells
that won't stop

growing, the lump
will kill the dog,

and every child walks away
thinking death is a dog
that can't be cut.

The Wasting

Landlocked in the hills
of Appalachia, far
from disappearing
coast lines, I did not
see the starfish suicide.
I read about it.
The Wasting, ecologists
called it, a disease driving
stars to rot, rip rays
from their own bodies. Sometimes,
a ray wouldn't know
it was dead, and would slither
away like a tongue.
What scared the ecologists
was the precision
of the self-mutilation,
the starfish like men
twisting, popping, throwing arms
from sockets. *Creepy*,
said one lab assistant, *just
fucking horrific.*
This gut language from one
used to speaking with
the eggshells of extinction
in her mouth—carefully, as if
talking to children
about death. It was, always,
children who noticed
the disemboweled stars washed up
on beaches, splattered
against the rocks in tide pools.
The adults didn't want
to bend knees, look closely.

Tripping Point

A kid fell here—in 1987, he thinks—Then another lady and her boyfriend in 2008—They had a suicide pact—Or maybe they were drunk, though the sign on the pine says ALCOHOL PROHIBITED—He's decided liquor turns people into idiots—Which is why the government hasn't outlawed it—Opiate of the masses, n'at—Up here, the air is cold, moldy—It's night—But he swears the sky looks red as grape skin—Some hours ago, he dropped three tabs of acid, and it's beginning to get weird—Not bad-weird—Just *different*—Not like the other times—*The trees are not hands*, he tells himself—*The trees are not hands*—His canvas shoes make no sound on the limestone boulder—Sweat dews his forehead—90 feet below, the forest hums with crickets—*The trees are not hands*—Eroded divots in rock hold puddles of rainwater—or are they eyes?—He submerges his pointer finger into one, retracts it quickly when a scream rips across the valley—Did his throat pulse?—He twitches, stumbles, the trees uncurling—Grasping—

I Talked to the Paleontologist

His job was to stare
into rocks and find the dead.
Usually, the dead were
trilobites, mosquitoes, ferns.
On Earth, the mass
of dead insects surpasses
the mass of our dead,
of *homo sapiens*—
"But we're catching up,"
he said. Microscopes
and curling fossils muffled
in theatrical
darkness, the room breathed
as if it were being
watched: slowly, so not
to alarm. "I found this
skull in Hell Creek," he gestured
at what must have been
a face, once, what had become
puppet propped on well-lit
pedestal. "Ever feel like
you're poorly put together?"

Sure, I said, nodding.

"Like a slight change in weather
could kill you, I mean
really knock you dead?" Yes. Sure.

It was the last time
I spoke to the man who stared
into rocks. Alone
at the funeral, I wondered
why I didn't read
the signs, the fault lines cracking
his eyelids. The way
even pins and strings couldn't
hold his bones in that
cold lab, an ice slab
melting in all directions.

Nearing Extinction

When it gets humid,
I bend my limbs around cold
boulders, the molars
spat out by ancient glaciers.

Geologic time
is not Romantic, but we
will still die in it,
soft spines fossilized like ferns.

Before going out
to prowl and drink, I comb
the Pennsylvania
woods. I find ticks. Lyme Disease:

An atomic red
halo circling a raised scab.
Like people on earth,
bacteria fight to live. This

is adaptation.
This is persistent motion.
This is a body,
a planet raging away.

After the Apocalypse

I will smash berries
into your mouth.

The berries will
be half ice

and half berry
plucked from a bush

sprouting over deer bones.
You will taste the deer

in the red berries.
You will grow

wolf's fur, triangle ears.
Your flushed skin

will be the color
of fruit, of insides.

Chewing,
you might remember

the rip and grind of machines,
the thick gray hours

of your work, how you watched time
ooze on the highway,

the subway, the sloppy way
you initialed all

paper. It will be too cold
to be Romantic

about the earth. We will snap
meat from twigs, the dead

will shoot up through us.

Hailing from North Appalachia, **Clare Welsh** is a writer and illustrator based in New Orleans. She laughs often and makes good hummus. Her writing has appeared in *McSweeney's, Back & Gray Magazine, The Chariton Review, The Susquehanna Review,* and *The Axe Factory.* To view her illustration portfolio, visit http://clarewelsh.format.com/. To view her blog, visit https://clarewelsh.wordpress.com

www.ingramcontent.com/pod-product-compliance
Lightning Source LLC
LaVergne TN
LVHW091235080426
835509LV00009B/1287